Made in the Image

Made in the Image

PLAIN POEMS

Joffre Swait

CANON PRESS

MOSCOW, IDAHO

Published by Canon Press
P.O. Box 8729, Moscow, Idaho 83843
800.488.2034 | www.canonpress.com

The following poems previously appeared in Joffre Swait's short collection *Well Met*: "Manna & Quail," "Thrice Beaten with Rods," "God Eats," *"Ave atque vale,"* "Batter My Heart," "Augustine Riddle," "The God of Pumpkin Pie," and "Thanks Forever."

Cover design by Zach Moll.
Interior design by Valerie Anne Bost.

Printed in the United States of America.

Library of Congress Cataloging-in-Publication Data forthcoming

23 24 25 26 27 28 29 30 31 32   10 9 8 7 6 5 4 3 2 1

Dedicated to my mother Carolyn
to my wife Kimberly
to my daughters Renata and Mara
to my sister Jennifer

✺ Contents

THE WORD

CAMEOS

PLAY & PICTURES

Plainly styled lyric is best.
Think on most days to test
Simplicity of pen.
So the kinder poets deal,
Who set the table for finest meal
And invite the reader in.

The Word

❧ Made in the Image

To wield a world, to work a deed,
To speak it soft or stern, at need,
Whether with much chanting, or cheering with delight,
Or thundering strength forth from the height,
This is to gods only given, and getting should be dear.

But the Lord of love, who allows no peer,
Has untwisted our tongues and tooled us new,
To wield our words and whole worlds hew.

Manna & Quail

"You shall eat until it comes out at your nostrils."
Numbers 11:18-22

Lord, all men must feed on words,
and poetry is our grain.
In a land that grows only wild rice
we ask for farms and rain.

Give us limericks for the happy times
and sonnets for the hot.
Give us meter when the forecast's good
but free verse when it's not.

Billy Collins is nice in the morning,
Eliot's for the afternoon;
Lewis or Hopkins are good with tea,
Kipling with a great monsoon.
But O Lord,
for your name and mercy's sake,
never give us William Blake.

If heavenly words are to be our diet,
there's all sorts of poetry,
and we'd like to try it.
But oh! lest our menu be all prose,
please, please Lord, please,
let not our poetry come out of our nose.

❧ Men at Church

Your fathers did not do the work,
Be jolly and be brave.
You have a task you must not shirk,
Be jolly and be brave.

Happy shall you be
That take and dash
Take and dash
Take and dash against the rock.
Do not close your eyes.

Be jolly, boys, and be brave.
But why are we jolly
And for what brave?
Jolly for what you go to,
Brave for what you shall come to.

Give thanks,
Weigh anchor,
Strap your packs.
Clean the sparkplugs and turn the key.
Yes, kick the tires and light the fires,
My jolly brave boys!
But why must we be jolly?
And why brave?

Jolly for the wars
And brave enough to come home.
Jolly for the assembly
And brave for the watch.
Merry for meeting
And steady for standing.

Do not close your eyes,
You jolly brave boys.
Sing another song
And pass the ammunition.
Praise the Lord
And chamber another round,
For it is better to be merry
Than to burn.

Do not turn from us, jolly brave boys.
Sing for us the songs of Zion,
Cry Harry and Saint George.
But how can we let slip the dogs
Of Saint George in a strange land?
But be jolly, boys, and be brave.

Blessed be the hour
You cinch your belts.
Happy the hefting of your glasses
And glad the gripping of your hammers.

Your fathers would not do the work,
But be jolly and be brave.
Clear the decks for what we go to
And what's to come.

Happy shall you be
That take and dash
Take! and dash!
Take and dash against the rock.
Do not close your eyes.

❧ Militant Times

The reason minor prophets are minor
Is this: that they weren't so big
They could talk of beating swords into plows,
Of not learning war anymore,
And see that peace is bought
By casting down not walls, but weapons.
Imagine all those people,
Shake your head a little ruefully,
For prophets who could actually believe
In peace through superior firepower.

The Confidence of Covenant Children

Step high.
Swing wide broadside,
Handsome and hopeful smile:
Lord-like my boys, little men with toys,
Be gods.

Swing low
And sweetly higher,
Make glad their heavenly sire:
Queen-like my girls, playing with mom's pearls,
Be gods.

☙ Thrice Beaten with Rods, and Baked into Bread

ἦθος ἀνθρώπῳ δαίμων

Is this the body and the blood for real
Or do I eat by sweat of wrinkled brow?
Feed on doubt and lust even as I kneel?

The words were spoken plain and bare as steel
But I would rate and complicate them now.
Is this the body and the blood for real?

There is no magic done to see or feel
Except a spelling of words in a woven vow.
I feed on doubt and lust even as I kneel.

Nor art nor philosophy make of it a meal
That does what's solemnly said. He never told how
This is the body and the blood for real.

Maybe it's animal weakness for social congeal,
The sodded quick of boiled bones' marrow
Where stew the doubt and lust even as I kneel.

But under this red rock is the new deal.
Not under; this rock's the whole loaf now.
It is the body and the blood for real,
Again I feed on bread and wine, and kneel.

❧ God Eats

Stephen was delicious because he was beaten,
tenderized by many stones,
his forgiveness-kneaded flesh
softened by killing blows.

Sharper than any butcher's cleaver
is the Word of God,
living and active,
piercing to the division of joints and marrow.
When finally pierced
between soul and spirit
he was made to be a perfect meal.

His God was a consuming fire
who devoured all his apostles
with delight, and smelled the smoke
of their burning as a sweet aroma.
Only their outsides were charred
as on a grill or cast-iron.
Their flesh was rare and easily cut.

Andrew and Peter were hung
upside down like pheasants,
left to age until perfect.
This is not to everyone's taste,
but monks and martyrs recommend it.

Paul was a work of art,
stricken, smitten, and afflicted,
tenderized several times.
On one single trip he was
marinated,
slow-cooked,
and injected with a fiery seasoning
designed to amaze.
Dry-aged then for two years
he was finally drained
and offered up quietly
without much to-do,
just as the sophisticates like it.
This is an excellent way
to prepare an older animal.

Only to a privileged few
does it fall
to be cooked over direct flame.
Most of us, like Paul, are allowed to get old.
Too old,
or perhaps it is simply a divine preference for brisket.

For your sake we are cooked
all the day long
in a little wine
which will finally break down

the tougher-habited sinews.
It's been a long time coming

But soon the great fork of God
will make your flesh
to fall tenderly off your bones,
the provings past,
the tastings done,
and you, served up
perfect.

❧ My Darling Sin

All her slain are a mighty throng. Her house is the way to Sheol.

I looked out through my lattice window and saw a foolish youth,
A man who'd left his sweet wife's pillow for a wanton woman's
noose.

At twilight in the evening dark, on a corner's hidden street,
Behold, the woman met her mark, then wiped her mouth, replete.

She seized him and she kissed him, said loud "I pay my vows.
To God I'm surely clean of sin, pray lie my couch right now."

All at once he followed her, an ox going to the slaughter.
Her brazen mouth she made demure, she trapped him when he
caught her.

I looked out through my window bleak and knew just what I saw.
For I had also left my wife to seek the temptress' maw.

My chamber's got a Darling Sin, I kiss her on the mouth.
I brought her home and locked her in, made a prison of my house.

If you end up on that woman's bed, when she is done with you,
O fly from there, and when you've fled, then go your vows renew.

Go sacrifice, and make a prayer, and plead for your God's grace.
Or Darling Sin will catch you fair, a prison her embrace.

We Are Not Alone

On the possible suicide by motorist of Randall Jarrell

When Randall Jarrell fell
Into the belly of the state,
When his wet fur froze,
When he was washed out with a hose,
I thought of rescuing Thunderbolts.

I know he wants me to think,
And oh, I do,
Of the machinations of states,
Of wheels within wheels,
Of cogs and hobnails.

I remember the twentieth century,
That even the most human were in it.
I remember the commissars, the drafts,
The Dresdens and Nankings.

But may we also remember the stories,
The songs about tin hats,
The little Jewish girl, the comrade,
The excellent monasticism
Of the ball turret gunner?

When Randall Jarrell fell,
He too thought of rescuing Thunderbolts,
Calling out to them:
"Little friend, little friend."

The Last Speaker of Sandy Point

On the Death of Cristina Calderón, Speaker of the Yamana Language

Hidden among houses not hers,
Last Speaker sits, silent.
This was all hers once,
Barely, before ever her birth.

Her people put on pelts
For the wet unwavering winds,
Which for layered lifespans
Spared them the Spaniards.

How many words there once were
To say stone on this island
She regrets to no longer remember,
As old as she is, as the spray and spew,

The gray and blue
Water, trees, sky,
Nothing beyond but the ocean
Her people never mastered.

Last Speaker is as dottered as documented,
By xenologists listed at length,
Linguists, missionaries, missionary linguists.
But they look no longer. She is the last.

There is no one to speak to. She sits silent,
Listless amidst the dwellings
Of this southern sea's masters,
Who smoothed the sea with their sails.

To her has been granted to hear
Over the warring of waters
A babel of tongues, Teutonic, Spanish,
And the Slavic of Sandy Point, yes.

There are more Croatians
On this island
Than ever were her people.

They build box homes corrugated and slat.
They board boats for big catches,
Wrestling in their nets enough new life
To feed not only their people,
But to ship it north,

To give life to the whole earth.
Its fish markets are fed
With Chilean sea bass, straight
From her people's cradle here,
The end of the world.

Cameos

❧ Friendly Aphorism

Friends have I by the hundred,
Friends I fetch by the penny.
Friends, where are you, I wondered,
For he has none who has many.

❧ Oenophile's Aphorism

The slothful
know the glow of merlot.
The tasteful
has a glaz of shiraz.

Holland

(Gay Pride Week)

I think that we should ride our bikes up and down the avenue.
We shall see a parade of dikes, packing paddles with no canoe.

A Song for William Blake

O rose
thou art sick,
to despite thy beauty
be such a prick.

❧ Onomatopoeia

These are words that sound
like what they mean:
bang, zoom, clap,
and (of another order)
ineffable.

❦ First Freeze

This year's first burst of cold
Brushed in brisk red the fringes
Of this street's less hardy trees
And yardling shrubs.

❧ Five Autumn
Pipe-Smoking Haiku

Each leaf has leapt
Willfully to be raked and piled,
Sweet smoke to heaven.

Autumn brings with it
A darker and ivy night,
The cool pumpkin air.

Full moon on the rise
And the going down of the same.
Porchsitting pipe smoke.

I wear a sweater
For the first time this season,
Shelter in lamb's hair.

Just as the forest
Decides to shed its fur
I grow my winter beard.

Play & Pictures

Ave Atque Vale

I meet a friend after work

Hail fellow, most well met,
I slap thee on the back and shoulder!
Here's ale bowls for thee to wet
Thy throat and whistle before you get older.
Long hast labored, and hast sweat;
Drink thou this beer, it gets no colder.
Then get thee hence, all free from debt,
Thy kids to kiss, thy wife, to hold her.

✌ Fiction/Non-Fiction

An argument's a trade.

An argument's a trade, it needs the other man.

He's hoping to get paid, you hope to pull the scam.

An argument's a story.

An argument's a story, it follows a straight line.

You load it on the lorry, and hope it's there on time.

Beginning with the Logos (A Sonnet for Advertising)

Un soneto d'amore per G. M. Hopkins e Wendell Berry

The Roman roads endure, and English trails

Still cut through Appalachians, axe and Indian.

How great are man's achieves, the engines and rails:

The whiskey-fueled Burmese, the grand Canadian.

But greatest yet, the wide and open flow

Of six-lane American brand-name roads,

Of neon, of franchise, and plastic signs in a row.

Beginning with the logos, enfleshed in gold,

These wide and brazen paths, all lit at night

Drown the stars above and block the trees;

But not one name, or center, or communal site,

Is known. All sprawled are the places we take our ease.

The tributary streets do not meet, but fall,

Separate, downtownless, to drink the malls.

A Church with a Graveyard

Death's chill church,
Stone-stopped and mute.
Graves greet you,
And grass,
At the door.

Death's chill church,
Stone-stopped and mute.
Graves greet you
At the door,
And earth.

🌿 Kudzu

*Old train tracks and a vine-covered hill from a busy new shopping
center below.*

Still train on trestle,
Still trestle train
Move me away to the South.
Move me to peaches
or in the low country, collards.

No more skipply erected
Busyness, no more poured progress.
Let me sit unmolded
On a new cut road.

I will labor.
I will cut a new road.
I will lay a new track
That moves me to peaches.

I will not tip the boilsome vat
To pour out river on river
Of six lanes.

Sit still on trestle, train.
Sit still and simply watch

As through your vine-covered hill
And under your steel-hatched body
Those six lanes run and run.

❧ Freedom in Form

In those days of sweater vests,
When men wore hats,
And children ties
With the top button cinched.

In those days without tennis shoes
Except for exercise,
In those days of *yes ma'am*
And *no ma'am* and get up
When she walks in.

In those days of closed air,
In that ancient day of rules
At work, at home, at play;

In those days of always deference,
When life was shorter, shorter and tighter;
In those days a man could light his pipe,
Or not, as he wished.

❧ Inkling

On reading Seamus Heaney's The Errand

The first time he read the piece,

Big-bearded and paternal

He saw the trinity of it:

The father with idea, bidding the son do,

And the son seeing the joke in it.

But the spirit, is it most easily

The level itself,

Is it a new tying of the tie,

Or is it more simply, less easily,

The light-filled smile between son and father?

❧ Salt of the Earth

The ham we treat with brine,
And then soak out the cure.
The bird in salt divine
We drown and then immure.

Festal foods we must exalt
With the liberal application of salt.

Bible Belt Blessings

Let us join this most sacramental of societies,
Sunday's society of beer and monster truck rallies,
Of kicking off this year's revival, of announcing next year's,
Of Sunday lunch as meat and three.

Let us think in a commonplace way
How this day of days,
This Sunday! Sunday! Sunday!
Has here in my grotesque country
Become the everyday, its wind pouring over
Into the Lord be with you, and with thy spirit.

❧ Apéritif & the Meal Thief

"La manzanilla de Sanlúcar y Los Puertos alegra a los vivos y resucita a los muertos."

The insurance salesman and process management consultant
Will tell you that it's best to trip light. Carry-ons, kid.
An acquaintance took bags to Rome, which with ancient
Tradition the natives stole while giving lodgment.
    Someone took my CDs in Madrid.

How like an avaricious hotel clerk
Is every meal you've taken in all your life.
Most dashed off some sugars, and tried not to work.
And you, complicit or embarrassed fell asleep to their smirk,
    And blamed your schedule, or maybe your wife.

The very best meals have worked to impress and to wow
The sleepy tourist who fatly steps to the table.
Because you travel heavy, with a weight on your brow,
The meal sneaks your time, your most valuable now,
    And sells to his cousin as quick as he's able.

It is wiser to travel as if eating a five-course meal,
To show up with an empty stomach and an edge for appetite.
If you're to eat the entire world with zeal,
To devour all they offer in Des Moines or Castile,
    Come wakeful-eyed, with spine upright.

Travel light to your meals. Check in no worries or cares.
Simplicity and joy are the carry-ons you need.
If you don't speak the language, listen and be aware.
Show up to the table ready, awake and *légère*.
    Let nothing be stolen from you while you feed.

If your palate is training, your start and first step must be bright.
Make yourself time to choose an apéritif,
Something dry and clean, to start up your tongue with light.
Calvados, or maybe champagne, or any wine that is white.
    Gin and tonic wakes your tongue before beef.

I remember the start a manzanilla sparked in my mouth.
This friend and I sat on the lawn, our wives cooking young,
Many years ago. He in Minnesota now, I the South,
Our first children were just babies, kept in the house,
    Our new lives on the tips of our tongues.

Which seems heavy, but tastes just like chamomile tea.
I still own that time, the little dry apples still carry
Lightly in the throat, an entire meal now free
To travel through time, not trapped by dull inattentive me,
    But wakeful once waked by a sherry.

Hilarity

❧ The Problem of Stoicism

Marcus Aurelius, when Emperor of Rome,
Sat down to write a stoical tome.
The famous "Decline" that Gibbon wrote down
Began when good Marcus took up the crown.
Whether in charge of the Thundering Legion
Or fighting on horseback in Parthian regions,
His mind, it was clear, was not on the bellum,
But rather on what he would next put to vellum.
It's what's bound to happen when you're the king
Of what you despise, i.e., physical being.
He first was a stoic, then a rex, in his heart.
But hey, at least they say he was smart.

❧ Batter My Heart

A Son Asks for Breakfast

Batter this griddle, thrice-blesséd mom; for, you
As yet but beat, sift, stir, mix the leaven,
That it may rise, stand, puff nicely to heaven;
So cook, and if it burn make it new.
I, like a besiegéd town, without my vittles,
Labour to patience, but oh, to no use.
Ham, and biscuit, coffee, orange juice,
Make me crave sorely; so dear woman, please griddle!
Dearly I love you, and would love to wait,
Yet am undone by the aroma of bacon.
So pour that batter, flip it onto a plate.
Soon brothers and sisters will smell what you're makin'.
I beg you to stack them in piles at least three,
I will never be fed unless you will feed me.

Deuteronomy 24:5

"When a young man marries he may not go to war,"
That's a rule the Scriptures had.
The duty that he carries before he hits the door
Is to make himself a dad.

Ancient Thirst Trap

I have chose some mother-of-pearl
As the tool to get me the girl.
Some say diamonds get the belle,
But I prefer the guts of a shell.

Chocolate & Chile

The Spaniard who discovered cocoa
Was driven quite nearly *loco*.
 He was served it with spice,
 Which he didn't think nice,
When it melted from his nostrils the *moco*!

Double-Dipper

There once was a man of Toulouse
Whose morals at potlucks were loose.
    He'd use, for example,
    A dirty spoon as he'd sample,
And taste with his fingers the mousse.

Law Limerick

There once was a prophet named Moses
Who dished out the Law in large doses.
    He said, "It ain't high
    Nor deep, it is nigh!
Nor as hard as thou supposes."

❧ Corinthian Supper Limericks

There is a young woman named Mabel
Who sits at the Christian table
    With no thought or care
    Toward her sisters there,
But drinks just as much as she's able.

There is a young man named Neal
Who sits to the Christian meal
    And eats to High Heaven,
    But not with the leaven
Of folks he could touch or could feel.

Riddles

Saint George is the saint of Anglic society,
He rescued the maid, slew the drake.
But he can't hold a candle to his colleague in piety
Who instead of a dragon did away with a snake.

There once was a man with a golden goatee
Who killed romish krauts in the north countery.
He lost his horse Streiff, a magnificent steed,
But he took it well . . . after all, he's a Swede.

We've just three hundred men in their mail
But with Yah on our side we'll not fail.
    We'll give out a shout
    And we'll drive Midian out,
Or my other name's not Jerub-Baal.

To the land of Woden and Thor
Came a man who is linked evermore
    To two pieces of wood;
    His name was Do-Good
And his story is Yule-time lore.

This Hippan just couldn't understand
How natural was evil in man.
  With his friends he did loot
  A pear tree of its fruit;
The motive was "just 'cause we can."

Answers: Patrick, King Gustavus Adolphus, Gideon, Boniface, Augustine

MADE IN THE IMAGE

For Public
Performance

∾ The God of Pumpkin Pie
A Thanksgiving Poem

The beasts of the forest all thank God in chorus
For the acorns all strewn 'neath the light of the moon.

The oak tree is king in the woods of the East,

Its roots reach down deep to the sky.

A flock of plump turkey passing through make their feast,

On them we'll the same with a sigh!

We'll eat turkey and pumpkin pie, my boys,

Turkey and pumpkin pie!

The boar roots and snuffles, the sow digs the truffles.
For the treats that they find they thank God who is kind.

The pigs whom we feed and tender our care

As there in their wallows they lie,

Are sweetest of meat and súrpassing fair

When cured off the rib and the thigh.

So it's ham and pumpkin pie, my boys,

Ham and pumpkin pie!

The beasts of the bog, the Boggart, the Frog,
And magical Man, how they love berry cran.

The woodpeckers, warblers, and wrens of the slew

Never thought in their time 'neath the sky

To mix sweet and tart in a red gummy goo

That the Maker of all glorifies.
So it's sauce and pumpkin pie, my boys!
Sauce and pumpkin pie!

The brewster or brewer, that fat barley stewer
Lifts hands up to heaven for grain and for leaven!

Of saints for all ales, either brewed or mirác'lous,
The church she has never been shy.
Even good old Saint Nick, and Saint Arnold the maculate,
Praised our Gód for unending supply!
So it's beer and pumpkin pie, my boys!
Beer and pumpkin pie!

You creatures of God, who dwell on the sod
You armies above, to your dread Lord in love,
From whom blessings flow to the high and the low:
Praise him who is great with a lift of our plates!

Our God gives pumpkin pie, my boys,
Our God gives pumpkin pie!

❧ Thanks for Ever

A Thanksgiving Poem

"But as for me, I am like a green olive-tree in the house of God: I trust in the lovingkindness of God for ever and ever. I will give thee thanks for ever, because thou hast done it; And I will hope in thy name, for it is good, in the presence of thy saints." *Psalm 52:8, 9*

I. Taking Time

Why do we mark out special time,
and why do we mark it with food, and with rhyme?
The Lordship of Christ's in all of history,
He enacts it through means, both obvious and mystery.
This poem's about good Jesus, our King,
And how he has made us right able to sing
Thanksgiving to him throughout the whole year
For taking away all our dooms and our fears.

This poem might get complicated,
So I'll explain how it's all related.

Adam was put in a garden sweet,
Where the fruit of the ground was sufficient meat.
All of the earth was his domain,
Even time was beneath his reign.
For God had made him not to die,
With eternal life beneath the sky.

But when we sinned we began to fear,

As seasons turn then death draws near.

Where once time meant more life with God,

Now time stalked, and ripped, and clawed.

The pagan man felt the trap of age,

That time and death were a bitter cage.

So Norseman, Greek, and the Chinese,

Said time was a circle, with no surcease.

The seasons and time would go ever round,

And crush all our cities to powder fine-ground.

Then Jesus came to make the world new,

The circle was broken, time was made true.

While earth and the seasons still cycle and spin,

Time marches toward her first goal in the end.

Creation anew, which came and which comes,

Brought a sense of time to his new Chosen Ones.

He's called us to climb up to his holy hill,

Sing thanks that he's saved us, is saving us still!

We now mark the year as Christians may,

By festival, feast, and by high holy day.

A humble spirit and grateful heart

For the spiritual food that He does impart.

This poem next will tell who hears,

Thanksgiving ends and begins the year

With gratitude for all his provender

As it opens and ends the Christian calendar.

II. *The Holiday*

Thanksgiving comes in autumn time,
which is the time of fading.
The glory of the trees is gone
and winter soon comes raiding.

And death has stalked us all for long;
death will still come creeping.
In winter man has need for bread,
and hunger finds him weeping.

In spring man watches skies for rain
and knows his life is set
On whether earth will grant reward
for labor and for sweat.

In summer all begins to grow,
the beasts and the diseases.
If death can close its awful jaw,
it never will release us.

And so the world will spin its course;
Adam counts the seasons.
The sons of Adam never make
escape, by force or reason.

But Jesus made the world brand new
when Jesus broke the ages.
Time had trapped us in a ring;
we now ascend, in stages.

We once were caught by time and death,
the seasons were our prison.
Now we climb the Holy Mount,
and sing that he is risen.

Now songs are what will mark our time
as we climb to be near.
Thanksgiving Day can summon us
to sing a festal year.

Thanksgiving comes in autumn time,
which is the time of reaping.
The glory of the fruit lives on
for the food that we are keeping

To feast and drink when Advent brings
Heaven's Bread to the table.
Winter comes, but we are warmed
by Creation in a stable.

All the beasts and all the nations!
They all may enter the store.
The winter brings Epiphany,
and nations stream up to the door.

Within that door the seed is kept,
At Easter it will flourish.
We the buried all rise up,
With manna we are nourished.

The fruit of summer rises up
in the time we named Ordinary.
Where once was jungle, now we find
Garden, farm, and dairy.

From there our summer leads to fall,
we've been fed from day to day.
A year has cycled fully 'round,
We sang ascent up heaven's way.

On Advent Sunday another year
will be marked out in song,
where every Sunday's a holy day
and festal weeks are long.

This new creation and new time
is a joy to the grateful.
We thank our God, who did provide
down to every plateful.

So this is where our verse can change,
and cheer our celebration.
America may thank our God,
the Church is his true nation.

Our fathers found, in hostile land,
an unexpected mercy.
And so do we, and just like they,
we feast upon a turkey!

   MADE IN THE IMAGE

So let us thank the one true God
for good gifts and for plenty.
Begin this year, now raise a cheer
in thanks to One for many.

III. *Thanksgiving for the Turkey*

We thank our God for the turkey who died,
For farmers from Georgia, and peanut oil.
It's fairly good baked, but it's better deep-fried
In a pot full of fat that's been brought to a boil.

These orange potatoes, which some have called sweet,
Were never named thus by we honest fellows.
To live up to their name, to be proper and meet,
We've added brown sugar, and also marshmallows.

We thank God for beer, this strong heady ale,
With which we toast health, and might come from Him.
Yes, sugar and yeast make beer hearty and hale,
As the wine of the Spirit gives vigor and vim.

So here is good health to the people of God
Who love him in every season and day.
For He loved us first, which seems a bit odd,
But now we're his children, so hip-hip . . . hooray!

We children will toast our great God, who is Father.
Mighty hen, we're his chicks, in his bosom we lay.
Creator of all, our Good Guide and our Rudder,
Sustains us each day, so hip-hip . . . hooray!

Again, let us cheer our strong God, who is Son.
Came down from Heaven, so that He may
Conquer our death, a fight that he won.
He's the first-fruits of life, so hip-hip . . . hooray!

Once more we'll cheer our swift God, who is Spirit.
He's given to us, and with us He'll stay.
A comfort, a joy, whenever we're wearied,
He'll never forsake us, so hip-hip . . . hooray!

So now raise your glasses, and encourage your neighbor,
With Thanksgiving cheer the God who gives favor!

To Father, Son, and Holy Spirit, let's drink our thanks!

Find more books on poetry and writing at

JOINCANONPLUS.COM

SCAN TO
GET STARTED!